The Frog Poem Project

The Frog Poem Project

Nicolette Costanzo

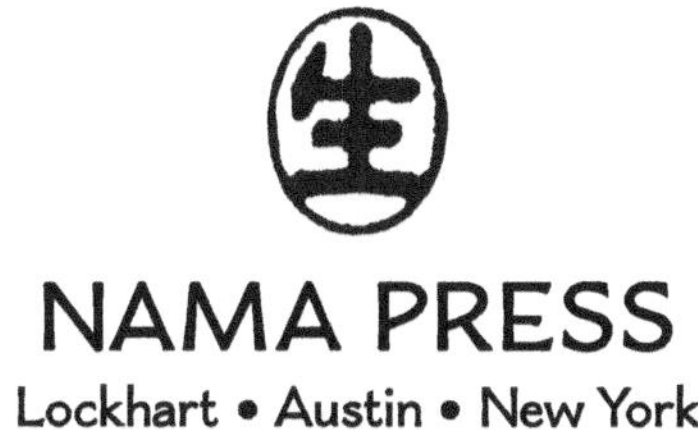

NAMA PRESS

Lockhart • Austin • New York

Sincere thanks to SEISMA Magazine: StudioLab, https://seismamag.com/studiolab, Spring 2024, where portions of The Frog Poem Project first appeared.

Nama Press
Lockhart and Austin, Texas & New York, New York

© 2024 by Nicolette Costanzo

Library of Congress Cataloging-in-Publication Data

Costanzo, Nicolette, 1974 –
The Frog Poem Project / Nicolette Costanzo.
ISBN: 979-8-218-50999-6 (pbk)

Manufactured in the United States of America
First Edition

Illustrations, Cover Image, and Book Design: Alice Lam, New York, NY
www.circlealine.com

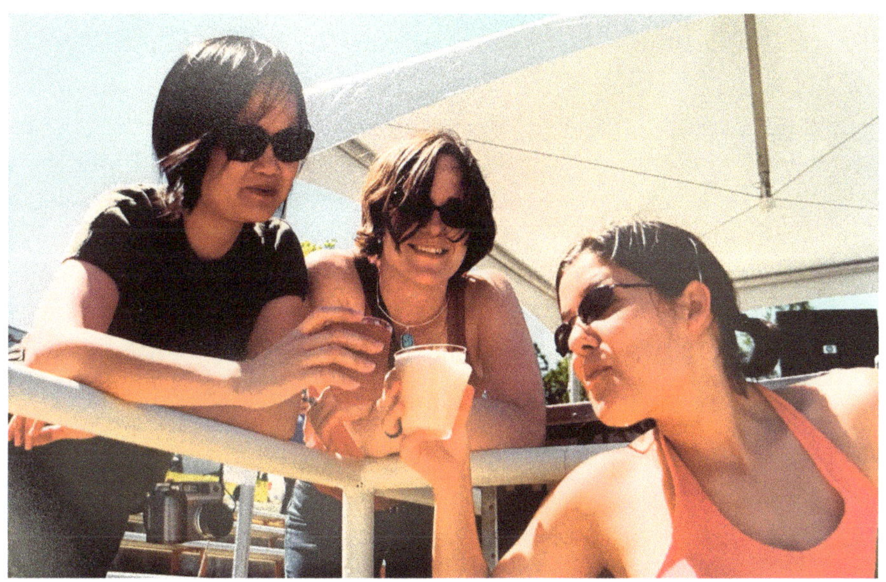

To the frog festival film crew: my lifelong best friends, Alice Lam and Kate Schubert, and my one and only, coolest sister, Valerie Rose Campbell. Your love, spirit, and energy to conspire and create sustains me. This project, and so much more, would not exist without you.

author's note

The following poem explores the language and pedagogy of frog dissection manuals, antique medical handbooks, and surgical gynecological texts. It was also influenced by visits to a human cadaver anatomy lab, and to frog festivals in Rayne, Louisiana, and Calaveras County, California. The illustrations are original and were created by Alice Lam, expressly for *The Frog Poem Project*. All anecdotes, presented under the heading *Leaps of Faith*, were spontaneously shared by the named speakers during conversations about the poem, as it progressed, and were written down at the request of the author. The preparation detailed in *Crispy Fried Frog Legs* was based on recipes in the independently published Rayne Chamber of Commerce Cookbook. All quotes, offset in yellow boxes to the right of the page, in dialogue with the poem, were taken from Michel Foucault's *The History of Sexuality*. Scenarios depicted in the classroom, the lab, and the medical establishment are based on real events.

contents

'attrekaphobia': a fear of frogs
frogs in my soup
frogs in my bed
crawling up my legs
frogs falling from the sky
what am I afraid of?

— Janet Cardiff
The Telephone Call, Video Walk
San Francisco Museum of Modern Art, 2001

When I was in preschool, we did a unit on life cycles. We went to a nearby pond, collected tadpoles, and kept them in tanks to watch them grow. I remember standing in front of my tank with my hand on the glass: inside was an impenetrable murkiness where thin black commas swirled. The impossibility of their legs bursting out their skin with webbed feet. Armless and fish-like they swam and grew. We drew pictures to chart their progress and some of the tadpoles had names but I don't remember naming mine. We watched our tanks and colored our pictures momentously, waiting.

And then they were frogs. Things that looked out from behind the glass making low burping sounds, moving with thick front trunks and sitting on v-shaped haunches. M. explained that frogs can't live in tanks, so we took them back to the pond and released them. Then we went to the butcher shop and bought frog legs. The preschool had a hands-on approach, so as always we made our lunch together. I don't remember clearly, but it must have been someone's job to wash the legs and dry them, somebody else's task to dip the legs in batter, etc. They were fried by the cook in the kitchen while we drank our milk and were brought out on large serving platters.

There were two legs on my plate, crusted, but still recognizable, and when the boy who sat next to me laughed, there were frog chunks in his teeth. Nobody seemed to realize what was happening so I screamed, *don't you get it? frogs! frog legs! we're eating frogs' legs!* M. told me to sit down, be quiet, and eat. But I kept saying it and soon everybody in the class was crying, throwing legs across the room, scooping half-chewed frog out of their mouths with both hands at once, jumping up and down, running in circles. M. was yelling threats, but nobody would listen or sit.

I was standing still, so it was easy for M. to catch me. She grabbed me by the shoulders, pushed me into a chair, tilted my head back, pried my jaw open and held it. Then she shoved frog legs down my throat. There were new screams and I heard a voice say, *stop it! you're killing her!* I couldn't move and it was hard to breathe.

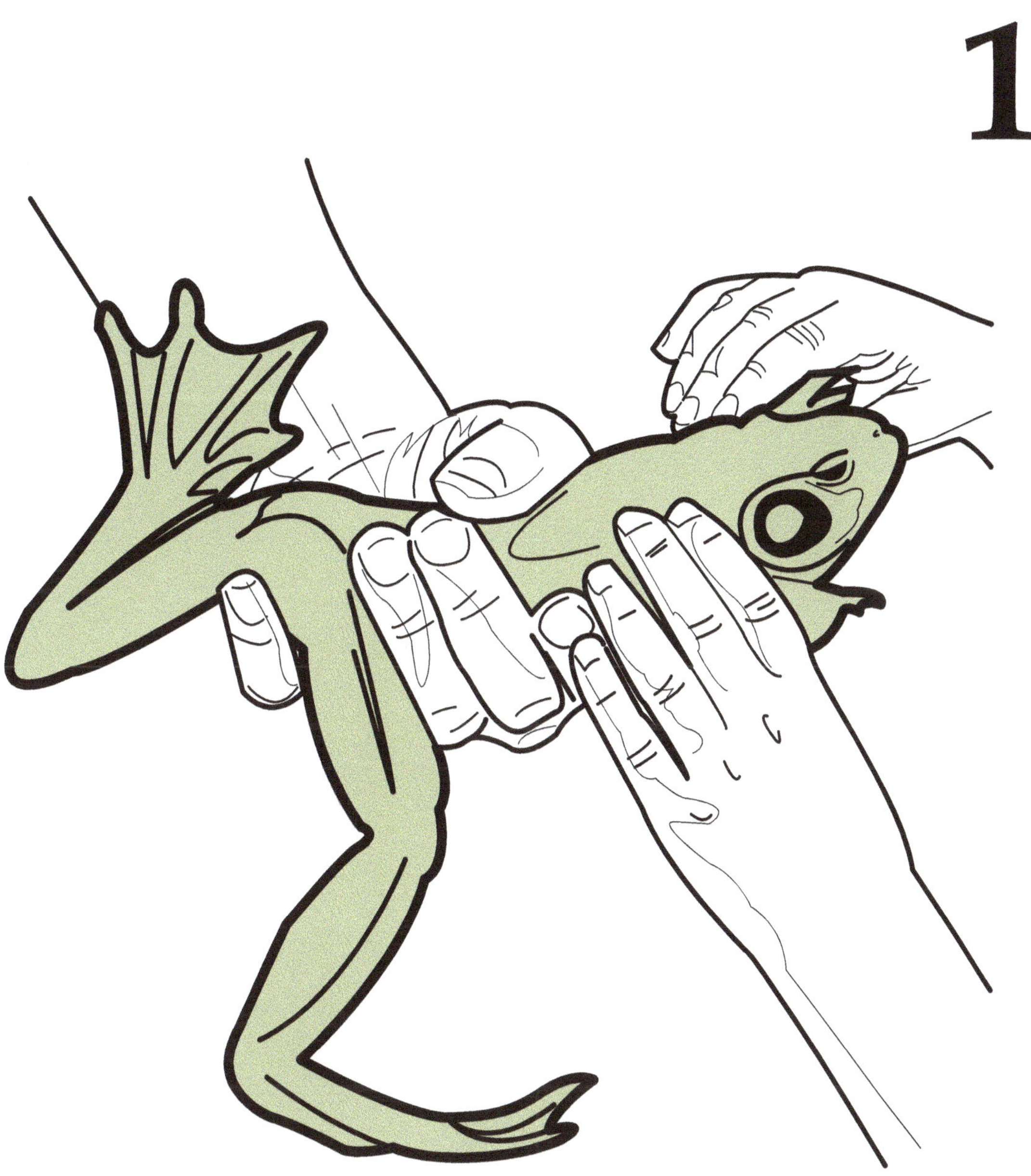

pa´tients (pā´shənts) *n* [*pl*] [[<L *pati*, endure]] **1** those bearing pains or trials calmly or without complaint **2** individuals awaiting or under medical care and treatment

on the examination table

sanitized but not sedated

your brain remains active

while your body lies shrouded

antiseptically silenced   modestly veiled

you wait to be seen

minimal   this room
fluorescent lights
glass jars on shelves
the corrugated ceiling tiles are pre-fab
and painted with stars

remember to breathe:

suck in extrusions   limbs   protrusions

skeletal rendering

lie flat

anatomical charts on walls
depict someone similar
but in a state you've never seen[1]

____

[1] before the doctor
     I am only one example of a body
     a felled tree in a forest   still rooted
     the circumference of my rings exposed

contemplate but don't crumple
your unblemished paper gown skin

suck in extrusions   limbs   protrusions

skeletal rendering

lie flat

the books say
there is a pattern   traced and pinned

but what if the cells are
fighting beneath the skin

a drama in juices

in lumps and fluid-filled sacs

Leaps of Faith

Alfonso was six years old when he died. He was running after the ice cream truck when a speeding car struck him down. He landed in his front yard; his crumpled body crushed like a bag of ice.

He was my friend. The one who saw me through my lonely pregnancy with his sweet smile pressed against my front screen door; all the colorful pictures he brought me and his little guy conversations that made me laugh.

Not long after his passing, I was bathing my new baby girl when I heard a curious laughter outside my window. I peeked through the curtain and recognized Alfonso's ten-year-old brother and a couple of the neighborhood boys, too.

When I saw what they were doing I felt sick; upset. Alfonso's brother had a bucket of frogs on the ground beside him. One by one he was pulling them out, placing a firecracker in their mouth and lighting them. The little bombs would explode in their mouths and burn their eyes out. The wounded frogs would leap away blind without a single sound.

In tears I ran outside and cried for him to stop, to understand what he was doing! Sadly, he stood up staring at me and my baby. He looked down at the battlefield of frog casualties, some unconscious; their beating hearts desperately screaming out from their chests. Tears puddled his mournful eyes.

That night (and many nights after) I slept restlessly; my head a fog of blind frogs trying desperately to find the right road home. Often I have to ask myself, "Does a frog have a soul?" I still wonder.

— Nora Barerra

knees buckled

    scalpel holds a sterile posture

ankles harnessed

    pretense of metal

the doctor says this time

    scissors emit their tinny laugh

we'll probe a little deeper

    cold silver bodies measure nakedness

navigate the insides

    exposure light its shine

according to a map

      calculate the lean

       heave a chemical sigh

remember to breathe:

raise diaphragm curtain

lower thoracic stage

raise diaphragm curtain

lower thoracic stage

raise diaphragm curtain

lower thoracic stage

in   out   in   out   in   out

keep breathing

an exhumed hand   a latex glove

commencement ceremony

a journey with unknown destination

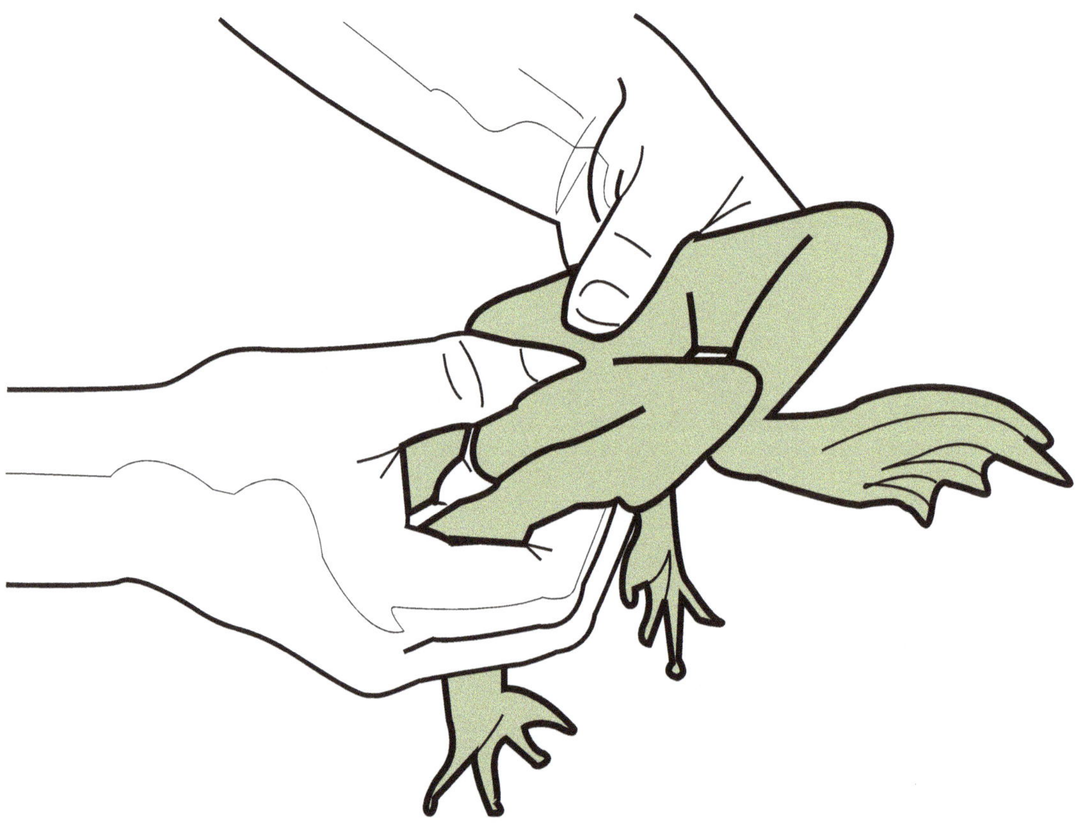

dis·sec´tion (dī sekt´zhən) *n* [[<L *dis-*, apart + *secare*, to cut]] **1** the act of cutting apart piece by piece, as a body for purposes of study   **2** an anatomical specimen prepared by dissecting   **3** a detailed examination or analysis

ranidae   rana

the frog is[2]

an amorphous pouch
peopled by long tiny bones

ribs in their cages

house

systems of juice-filled organs

                                        cellular symphonies

categorical infinitives

carefully laid   in the pan

---

[2] a reason for festivals and derbies
selected from buckets of water
at the back of the stage   set for performing
animal athletes   competitve jumping

Leaps of Faith

Preferably, the science teacher will be missing one arm. He will also have red hair and be slightly caustic, bitter, and mean. The frog arrives on a tray, possibly sedated? In either case, it's been in refrigeration, and so moves slowly, being amphibious and cold-blooded. You are also handed a tool that looks like a long needle with a handle. Your lab partner waivers, unable to kill the frog (even though they "take care" of the excess kittens on their farm by putting them in a plastic bag and gassing them with exhaust from their truck, no joke. They also have a really mean mutt who bit you on the leg once). So you take the needle and shove it into the frog's brain, around the place where you figure the brain must be. Then, you move the needle around in a circular motion, scrambling the brain. Immediately, the frog starts bleeding, and the kids around you laugh and point, because you seem to be the only one in the lab whose frog is floating in a pool of blood. Maybe you were a little too vigorous, but you really wanted to make sure the poor thing was brain dead before you started cutting it open. Supposedly, this process deadens the frog to sensory perception, the equivalent of a brain dead human who still breathes and kicks. It's hard for you to accept this fact though, even as you slice the frog's belly open and look within. This is a female, with her yellow egg sacks clearly visible. The lab teacher hands you all sorts of cool stuff to test on the frog; caffeine and other stimulants make the frog jump, or make its tiny heart beat very fast, especially when you put the shit right ON the frog's heart. To keep the frog still, you have to pin its skin to the Styrofoam tray at four points. At one point, the frog still jumps, propelling the tray across the counter and making the girl next to you scream. After lab, the frog goes back into the cooler, so you can operate on it again the next day (still alive, of course). I always remember operating on things in lab with a vague horror.

— Noel Kalenian

the frog has no neck

and is flat-chested[3]

transparent to the trained eye

each has the propensity to be

malformed   riddled with tumors   under siege

punctuated by hysterical openings

---

[3] neverthless picked to participate
   in one town's annual beauty pageant
   human/amphibian pairs dressed in matching gowns
   inert and on display
   pinched under the ridge below the head   across the back
   unwitting but abject contestant partners

trunk follows head
arms and legs extend
all directions identifiable:

        cranial

        caudal

        dorsal

        ventral

        lateral

        medial

        proximal

        distal

sacs within sacks

bones cross-hatching bones

a body

is a vehicle for deconstruction

hold disparate neon parts

evacuate the middle

reduce   deduce   to pieces

forceps   scalpel   needle

eye-dropper pipette

turn the page   peel the skin   begin

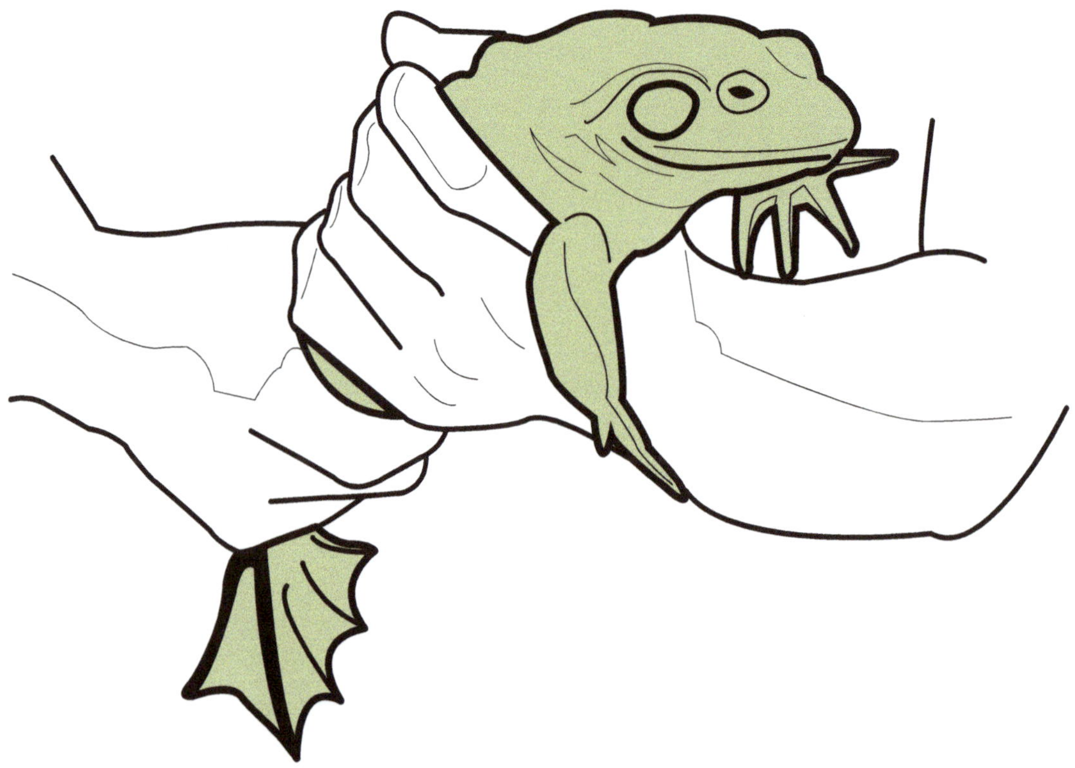

pri·vates (prī´vəts) *n* [*pl*] [[<L *privus*, separate]] **1** enlistees of the lowest rank   **2** the genitals: also *private parts*

sex by comparison

self defined by the presence of other

a productive and worthwhile use for dead animals

adolescent urges   rapidly changing emotions   sexual thoughts

organs in a similar position to ours provide insight

dexterity developed through manipulation of a specimen[4]

physical confrontation in a classroom setting

not just a figure of speech to suggest resemblance
contained   embodied   this metaphor

---

[4] I don't want to participate   but I'm forced to watch

        autoerotic activity   psychosexual fertility   reproductive muse

evaluate pubertal development

                the ovisacs distended with eggs

                              pressed in jelly

inner cyclical changes

cream-colored testes

            ball sac
            hanging outside the body

                     tender and smooth

oriented for easy access

in most extant organisms

a swollen base   with style   often sticky

stigma of various shapes   secretory structures

filament with a two-lobed anther at the tip

collective instinct   one's own volition   the pressure to perform

pleasure mechanics

arouse   arise

arrive quickly

through the flat expanse of lava fields

the epiphany of a sudden mountain range   astronomical

estrogen   testosterone levels peak

squander squamous cells
residue of projected papillae

corpus albicans   endometrium   vestibule

dull ache   discomfort   genital buzz
lining shed   hormone levels drop

eggs pass through

it takes energy to move fluid

a storage vesicle   a fringed tube

this pleasing passage

plenitude of the possible

secretions shoot

a characteristic odor
clean and moist

                                milk-white   clear   slippery

composed of thirty-two different chemicals
more than twenty amino acids

urogenital: reproductive and urinary
modified sweat glands

                        tiny ducts

                                      fimbria frayed and swaying

two glands   filled with tightly coiled tubes

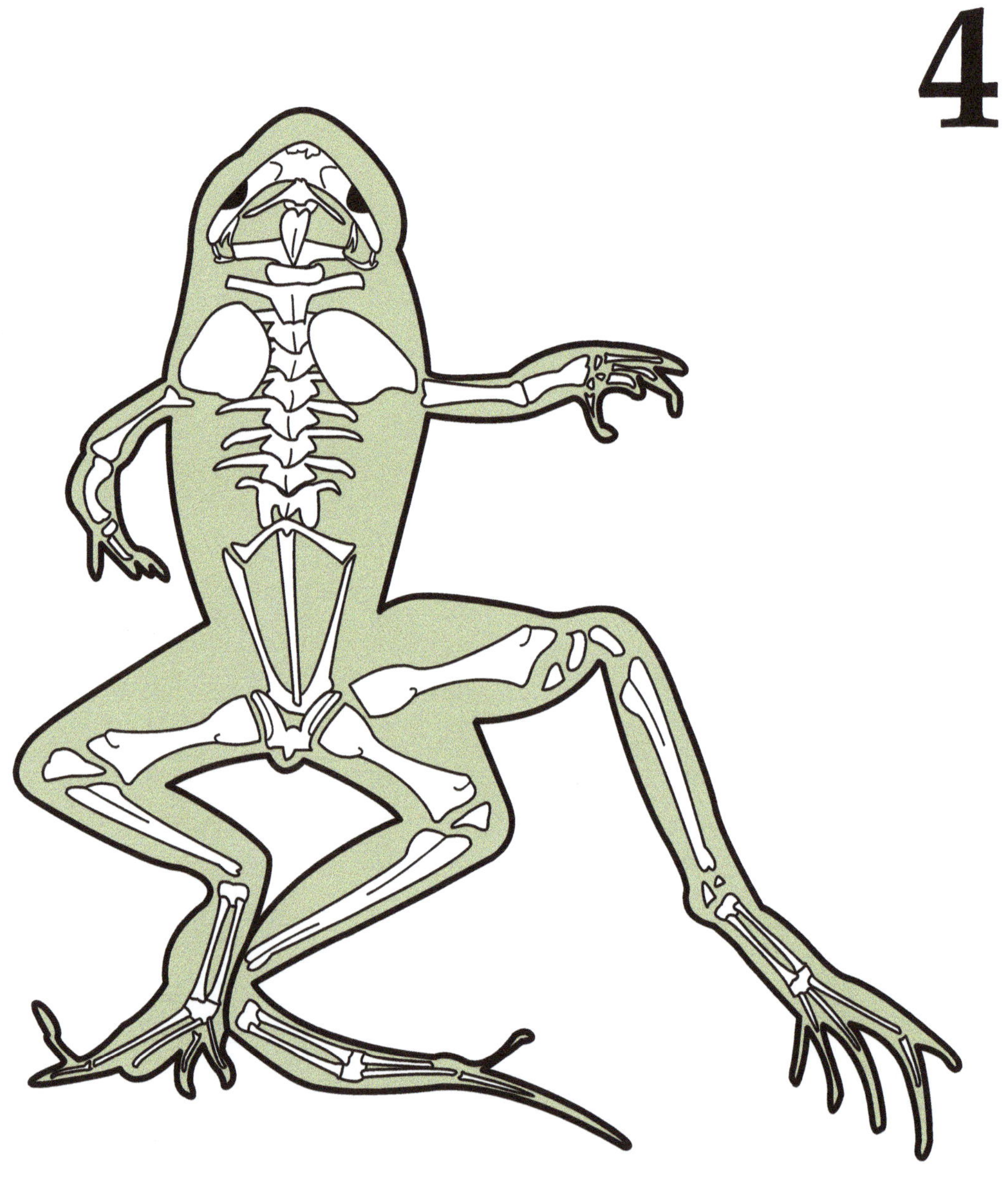

dis·ease (di zēz´) *n* [[<OFr *des-*, DIS + *aise*, ease]] **1** illness in general **2** a particular destructive process in an organism; specifically, an illness **3** a state of discomfort

Req. # 137778   Medical Record # 104061

Your recent examination showed an abnormality that requires further follow-up
by your physician or other health care provider. Please be aware that most of these
findings are not found to be malignant. You and your physician or other health
care provider will decide what additional tests are needed.

If you are not contacted within 7 working days or if you have further questions,
please call your physician or nurse practitioner.

Radiology Department

Contact your local facility for information.

a feverish wind
santa ana fire   sahara breath
arrested the pulse takes flight

or early frost
heat wave shift   moist skin
cloud-rubbed   face drawn
lined in pencil

respirations first shallow
then deep and gasping

body ashen suddenly ashen

organs a tropical storm

an accident   a fall   a sudden threat to the system

nauseated   needful   nonspecific
the body collects waste
grows mold

bulbous lump on an underside

ultraviolet radiation

persistent fever / unshakable cold

consumption

a spot turns bumpy

threat to habitat

a cut won't heal

pollution plays its part

a routine examination yields questionable results[5]

---

[5] fibrocystic breast disease
fibrocystic breast disorder
fibrocystic breast changes
fibrocystic breasts

technically the semantic shift is recursive
words falling into disuse   terms discarded over time
but my body is the keeper of every sentence
the sediment of each iteration accretes
aberrant is not a condition that disappears or resolves itself

Leaps of Faith

All of Matt's instruments of torture came from my uncle's shed, which sat behind the house and was connected to a large square of concrete with a basketball goal at one end. One night when I was visiting, we went out into the yard and caught a dozen frogs that were already headed toward the porch light. We easily snatched them from the grass and clasped their heads firmly between our index and middle fingers. We then walked them over to the basketball court, where Matt had laid out a coil of rope, an aluminum measuring spoon, a baseball bat, and a can of gasoline. He cut a long section of rope and attached one end to the rim of the basketball goal, letting the other dangle at chest level. I clumsily handed him our dull-witted, kicking prisoner. He took the measuring spoon, and in one swift motion, whacked the frog across the head and knocked it unconscious. He laid down the spoon and tied the legs of the frog to the rope with a crude double knot and let it dangle. While it hung there, almost invisible against the darkness like a rogue ornament or a warlord's trophy, Matt picked up the can of gasoline and unscrewed the cap. The gasoline rolled off the frog's limp body and spilled onto the concrete below, splattering onto our shoes. The very smell implied bad things.

"OK," he said, focused and businesslike. "Check this out."

He reached into his pocket and handed me a box of Ohio Blue Tips. I took one out and waited until he was ready with the baseball bat, which I was told was my cue. Matt got in his stance — I think his hero then was Jose Cruz — bat over the shoulder, hands gripping the tape high on the barrel. He was ready. I struck the match and gently touched it against the frog, then jumped back as it disappeared beneath a soft shroud of blue and orange and yellow flames. Matt waited until the fire reached the rope, and just when it was about to snap from the heat, he stepped high and swung the bat, sending the frog sailing into the darkness like a blazing roman candle. That night, we took turns seeing who could send them into the yard the farthest.

After a couple of years, our methods gradually became more cruel, almost medieval. One night we chased them down with crowbars. Another time with slingshots. Once, we were so out of options we simply impaled them with a steel grill brush. Until one day, when I came over and was told that there were no more frogs.

"They're all gone," he said, as he shot baskets near the shed. "I haven't seen one in two weeks."

I never knew what happened to the frogs. I suspect we killed them all, or perhaps they became smarter than us and simply stayed away. Back then I hoped for the latter. Because Matt was two years older than me, he soon grew out of killing. No junior high girls wanted to hear about lopping the heads off frogs with a crowbar. But as for me, it took a few more years.

— Bryan Mealer

the morphology of the malformation

does not define the cause

restless   thirsty   unnamed

systemic pressure falls

the itch disintegrates

pulse crawls

unit of illness   +   scepter of dissent   =   coldfront of fear

beat rapid   uneasy   compressible

unsex the funicular veins

the body is barometric

skin permeable and absorbent

- ☐ small head
- ☐ small eye
- ☐ displaced eye
- ☐ eye missing
- ☐ iris abnormally colored or shaped
- ☐ iris missing
- ☐ short jaw
- ☐ curved jaw
- ☐ jaw missing
- ☐ protruding tongue
- ☐ tongue missing
- ☐ spine extended beyond rump
- ☐ lack of an organ
- ☐ hunched back
- ☐ multiple complete limbs
- ☐ multiple split limbs
- ☐ limbs missing
- ☐ no elbow
- ☐ no hand
- ☐ no knee
- ☐ short bones
- ☐ extra digits
- ☐ short digits
- ☐ digits missing
- ☐ partial foot
- ☐ no foot
- ☐ short toe
- ☐ toe missing

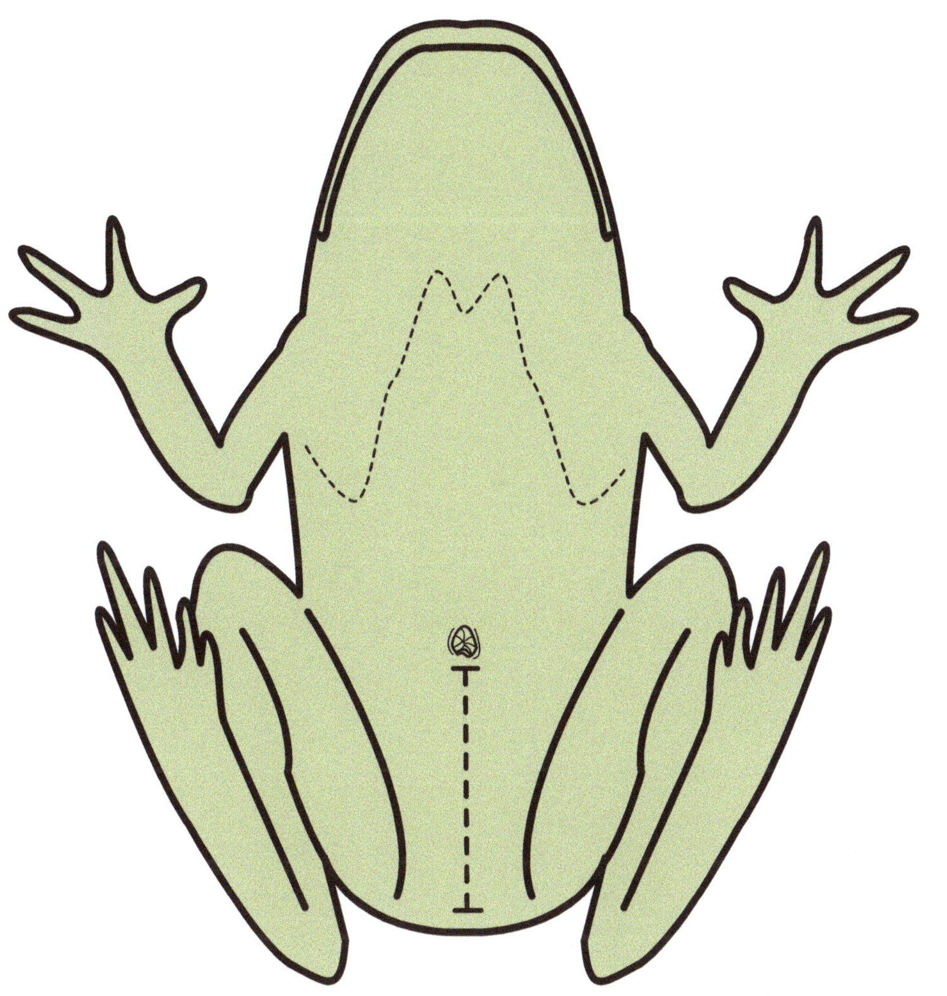

o´pen·ing´ (ō´pən iŋ´) *n* [[OE]] **1** a place of entry; portal; hole; gap   **2** a clearing   **3** a beginning   **4** the start of an operation

toe tagged and numbered

zipped up in bags   wheeled in on carts[6]

exsanguinated and silent

subjects bound like books

non-circulating   clutched at the spine

indefinitey retained for research purposes

---

[6] in the anatomy lab
    men are full body and on gurneys
    but women are reproductive parts only
    stored on a shelf

latex gloves stripped from a cardboard box

extricate multiple hands

the zipper is stiff but finally gives
an odor retaliates   pressurized air

a jar freshly opened

lotion   that has never been touched
preserved bodies
emitting their precise scents
chemicals pressing at the barrier of skin   seeping in

imagine the legs

how they must have buckled   the first time
see how still they lie

a road´s dead end
a finished sentence

how flat

laid out on platters
almost too tender to touch

arms wrapped in ethereal gauze

eyes find a rigid limb   its meat

the blade finds smoothest entry
navigates its instinctual path

umbilicus to symphysis pubis
caudal end to pectoral girdle

a shallow scalpellic slit

cut through skin and fat backing

north to jaw

up each arm   down each thigh[7]

southwest   southeast

to each knee

follow the paths of creek beds

scissors like mattress springs creak

follow the dotted lines

---

[7] I held a dead man's penis in my hand

loosen skirt from underlying muscle

peel back with forceps

lift

how thin this veil of skin

and pin

inside   the organs are like ripe fruit

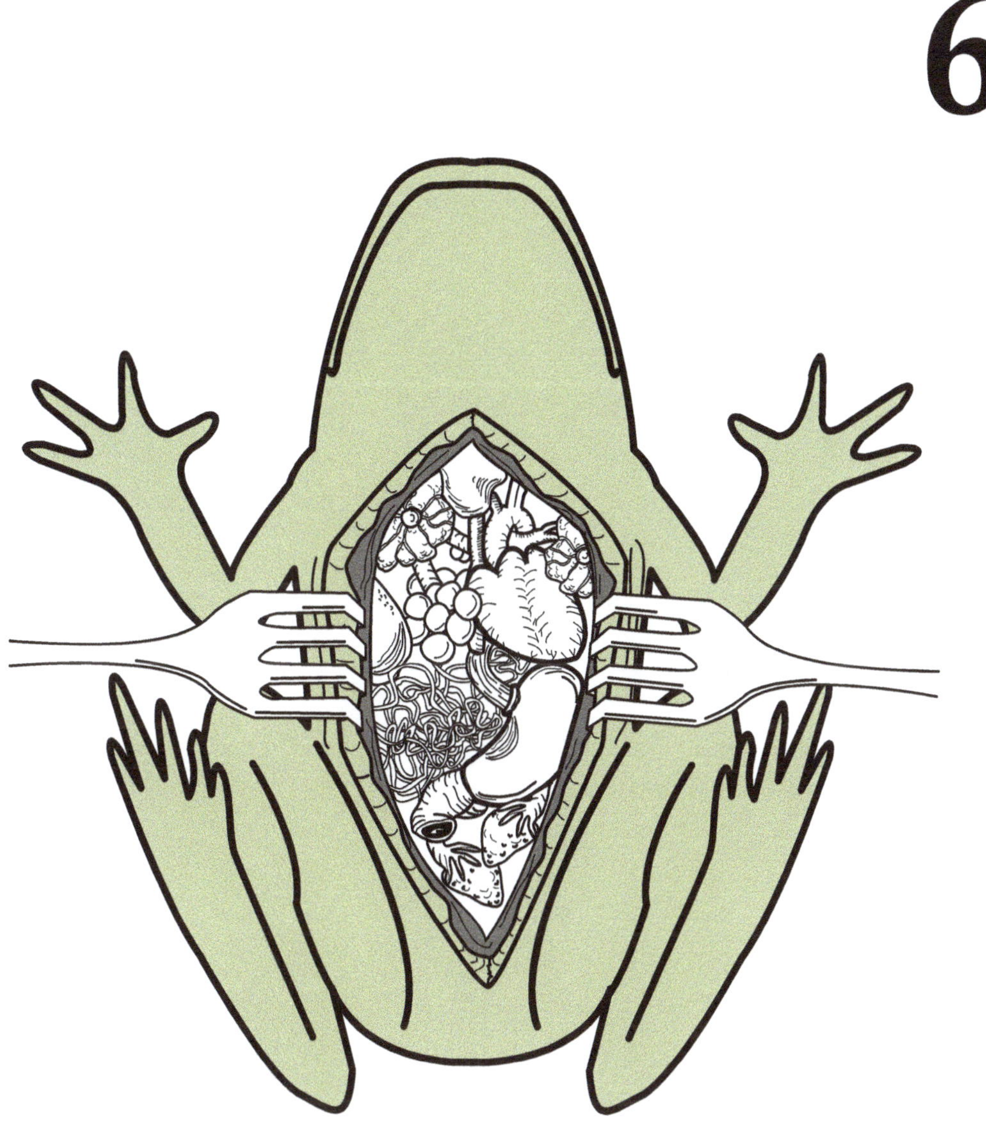

in·sides (in´sīdz) *n* [*pl*] **1** the interior or internal parts or places; the parts within **2** [Colloq] the viscera, entrails –*adj* [*s*] **1** internal **2** known only to insiders; secret

skull cracked   the head collapses

brain bearing weight
and architectural design

brow furrowed   smooth
chin bristled with whiskers
tongue a swollen gray member
stuck between teeth and cracked lips

breast plate unhinged

the heart is quantifiable on the scale

heavy in hand

when removed from its vacuous cavity
trunk proper

inside the hallowed sanctum   reside
the secret gems

a kidney so distinct

liver a lone mountain range

spleen still full

organs in the grip of chemicals
resisting atrophy   stew

cardiovascular passages

teeming rivers

stomach on its string

intestines rest in accordion folds

note muscles
well-formed and sinewy
ziphisternum to depress
linea alba   pelvic girdle

tubes like straws

musculo-cutaneous veins shockingly blue

ligature the intestines with thread
isolate the body wall and remove

score small mid-fascia
with the blunt end of scissors
push rectus ventral   dorsal

excavate caves   clear crevices stuffed with tissue

Leaps of Faith

As sophomores in high school we had our first dissection experience. Ours involved a frog that we etherized first in order to observe the still-beating heart and functioning organs. The observations and lab activities required of us were quite extensive, and not everyone finished during the allotted lab period. A few unfortunate ones had to return to the classroom after school in order to complete the job. My friend Rainbow and her lab partner Dan were subject to this fate.

I came to the biology room to pick Rainbow up a couple of hours after school ended. The room had an extraordinary smell to it that afternoon, a scent I couldn't place. Rainbow and Dan were hunched over the lab counter at the far end of the room, obviously frazzled and annoyed. The frog was splayed between them. In the case that students had to return to finish the dissection after school, there was a specific protocol to be followed involving the specimen. The frog was placed in the freezer until the students returned, at which point they were responsible for "thawing" it out using the microwave. Clearly, at this point no organs were functioning and the integrity of the lab was seriously compromised (as the teacher reminded us throughout the class period — looking pointedly at those who took more time than others). When Dan and Rainbow arrived to finish the lab, the job of "thawing" was delegated to Dan. At this time in high school, Dan was not only a shy and somewhat sheepish adolescent, but he was paralyzed by his crush on Rainbow. This may have led to his inability to focus on his task that afternoon. I walked over to them, noticing a cold silence between them and an unusually dark and crispy frog.

Rainbow looked up at me, glowering, and before I could ask she announced, "Dan cooked the frog."

— Rachel Mercer

Crispy Fried Frog Legs

12 meaty frog legs
1 1/2 c buttermilk
salt and pepper to taste
2 medium-sized eggs
1 tsp mustard powder
1 1/2 tsp Worcestershire sauce
1/2 tsp tarragon (optional)
1 c cornmeal
1 c sifted breadcrumbs
vegetable oil for frying

Snip off tailbone at top of frog legs and separate at the joint. Wash legs thoroughly in ice water, place in a bowl topped with 1 cup buttermilk, and soak in the refrigerator for one hour to tenderize. Remove legs from buttermilk and pat dry with paper towel. Season using salt and pepper and set aside. In a separate bowl, combine remaining buttermilk, eggs, mustard powder, Worcestershire sauce, and tarragon (if using). Stir until blended. Mix up cornmeal and breadcrumbs in a paper bag. Dip frog legs in egg and buttermilk mixture and drop into bag, 2 or 3 at a time. Hold bag closed tightly in fist and shake vigorously to coat legs completely. Heat vegetable oil in a cast-iron skillet. Place coated frog legs in skillet, close but not touching, and fry until golden brown, turning often. Take care, as legs will become more fragile as they cook. Blot crispy fried frog legs on paper towel and present on a large serving platter. Serve hot.

check tissue forceps

                                                pick peritoneum high   higher still

search the umbilical sky

                                        the bladder floats like a cloud

in this vast sea avoid pelvic adhesions
loops of bowel

                    what the nails sink into   *what striking the metal can bring*   *making the metal sing*

insert finger probes
draw laterally to view adjacents
palpate all around:

                                      with caution   avoid bladder   approach pubis

spinal cord spliced
each spongy lung removed
eventually   to increase visibility
the pectoral girdle will uproot

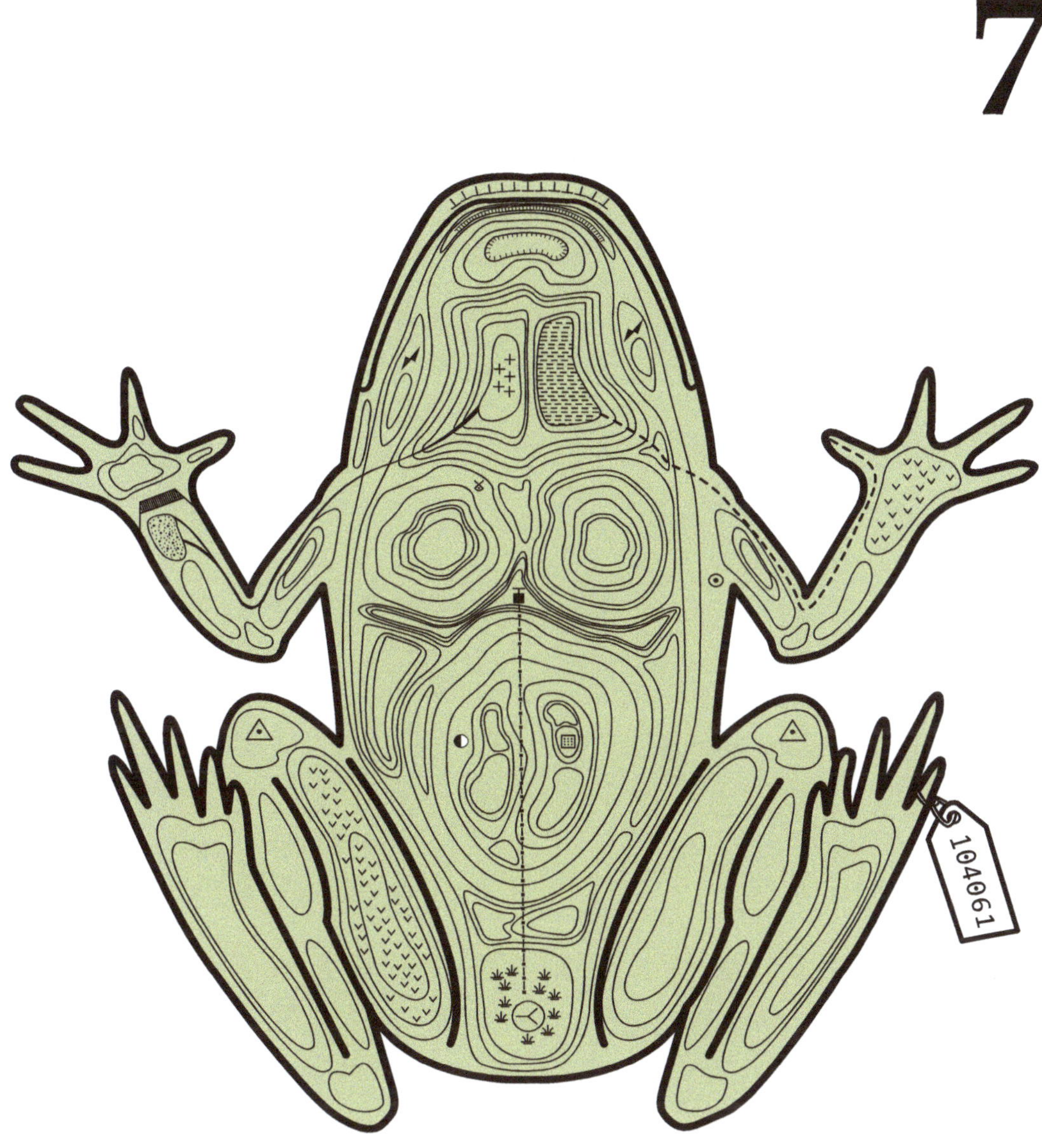

ren·der·ings (ren ́dər iŋz) *n* [*pl*] [[<L *re*(*d*)-, back + *dare*, give]] **1** reproductions by artistic or verbal means: DEPICTIONS **2** that which results from a process of melting down (fat) **3** residue or imprints left behind from the action of a repeated process

the body prostrate

is a diagram in three dimensions

a story written in code[8]

                  detailed in skin

                         pock-marked and dimpled

                         mottled and leathery

                    wrinkled   creased   calloused   rubbery

easily peeled   welded to fat

tattooed   pierced   cut   burned

                    retaining knots and spots

                    and some thick stitches

---

[8] I grow up in a town
criss-crossed by dry creek beds
torrents in wait erupt in a flash   flood warning
low water crossing
spawning ecosystems in the dredges as the deluge recedes
I write a song called *ode to roadkill*
to commemorate the remains
that populate then melt into the gravel on the street

Leaps of Faith

My street was not a highway, but a busy thoroughfare for the residents of about forty beach cottages on the oceanfront. Busy as it was, the street was also home to hundreds of frogs — called bufos (maybe for bull frogs) in the local English — and they didn't fare well on that street, frequently squashed and flattened by cars passing at night, when they, the bufos, were out and about. During the day, their flattened carcasses dried in the sun, and, after a few days of baking, kids in the neighborhood would pick them off the street and wing them like Frisbees. I had been working on the chemistry of ceramics glazes for a few months, experimenting with the colors achieved using different minerals at high fire temperatures — cone 9 +. One evening, it occurred to me that the bufo remains would have a lot of iron, calcium and some other minerals, and, surveying the street for 100 feet in either direction, I realized I had an abundant natural resource of frog bodies to experiment with. I filled two five-gallon buckets with bodies beyond the first stages of decay, built a fire on the beach, put them in a huge cast iron lidded pot and burned them to ashes. I mixed the ashes with a binder until the mix was the consistency of lumpy oatmeal, and, the next day, applied it to a series of thrown forms — large vases, bowls, and plates. A few days later I got space in the kiln and fired them to cone 10. The glaze was a spectacular layered mix of deep chocolate brown and gold with green drips and spotting.

— Paul Eveloff

a frog yields its white belly

prophetic   confessional

exposure to the elements

climate change   contaminated water   polluted air

leave visible traces   irreversible

repercussions manifested destroy systems

there is evidence in the figure   lines on a form

this one haggard

this one beaten

this one suffering a blow

to the head

this with skin thinner than the rest

while the mind may induce amnesia

light born when a tunnel breaks

somatic disturbances   spaciness
a feeling of unreality

the body knows no lie kept fresh

lime just squeezed
lemon too soft

a blemish   a scar   a plastic hip replacement
an inventory of lumps and bumps and deep tissue bruises

it comes whispered

in solemn tones
on formaldehyde breath

in the dream

all the people are suddenly naked

in the dream

there is a jungle of shadows
tissues separating from their fibers   membranous

movement through water

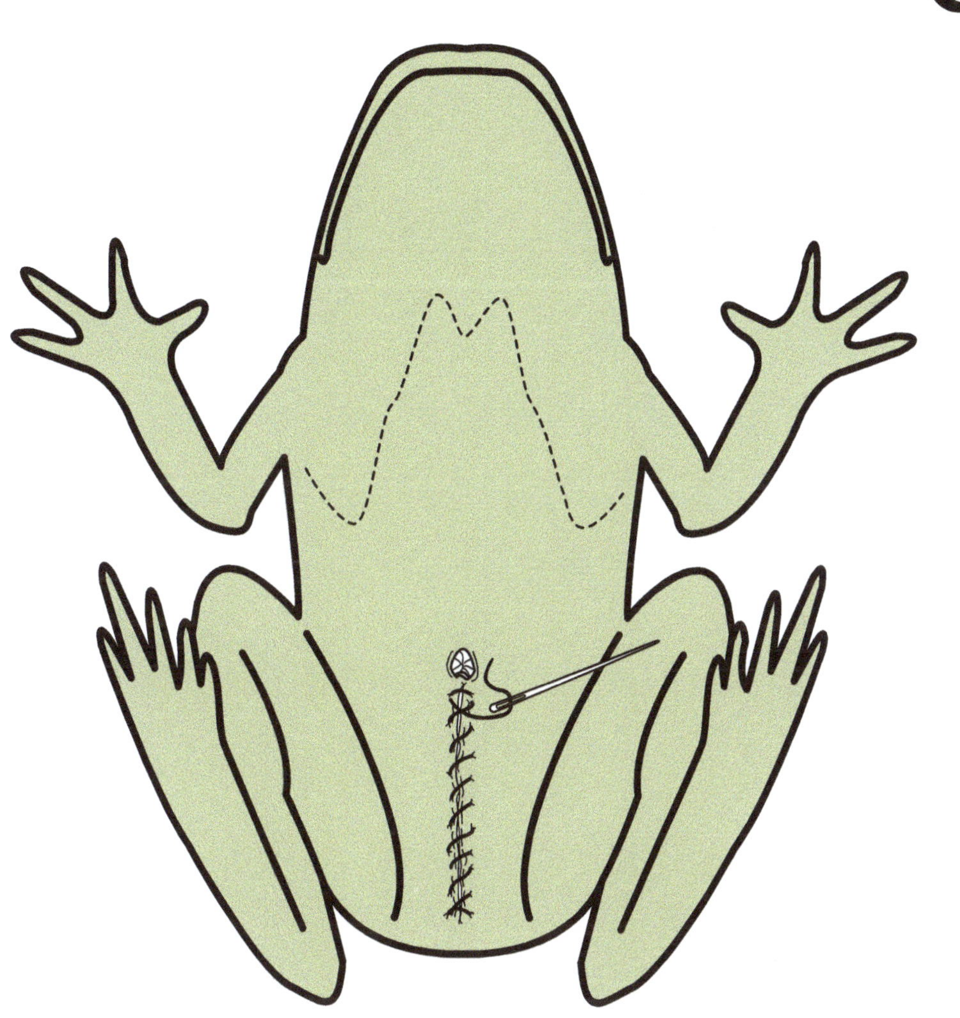

clo·sure (klō´zhər) *n* [[<L *claudere*, to close]] **1** an act of closing: the condition of being closed   **2** a finish; end   **3** something that closes <pocket with zipper ~>   **4** the ending of debate by immediate vote

ritual resolution

nails extracted from walls
holes filled with putty   sanded smooth
a survey of the nether regions
yields a map

relief and proportion

sound waves define a path

echo

a destination
vistas merge at the horizon   a line
scar across the sky goes black   contusions dissipate in blue

black silk at first bite

begin stitching at the top of the wound

dip   pierce   and pull
dip   pierce   and pull

after the fall

picking up the pieces
everything has its place to return to

surgical gut   surgical gut   the peritoneum is closed with

O O chromic surgical gut

down from fascia

up from pubis

two threads find their common   and tie

since skin is thin
approximate in silk or metal clips
stack vertical mattresses[9]

---

[9]

vertical mattress stitch:
needle through skin
through fat cut right
needle through fat
through skin cut left
needle nick tiny
left   right   tie

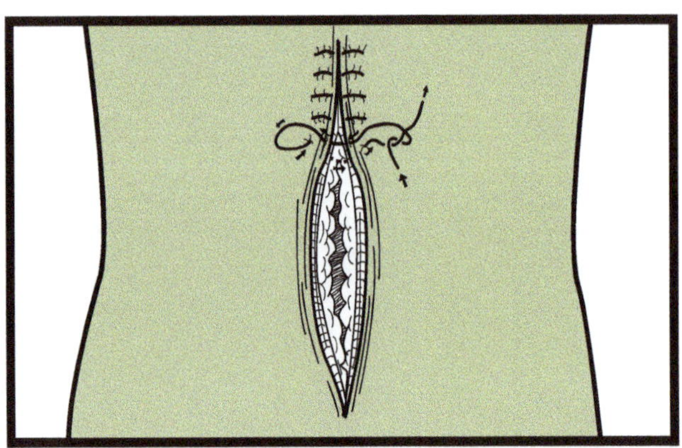

senses shrouded in fog
passage through sedimentary states of being
under revolving moons

tingling

presence returns to the limbs

red backs of eyelids

steady ray of the surgical lamp seeps through

veins find their pulse
heart recognizes a familiar tune
cap screwed tight   book snapped shut

extracts stored on a shelf for later use

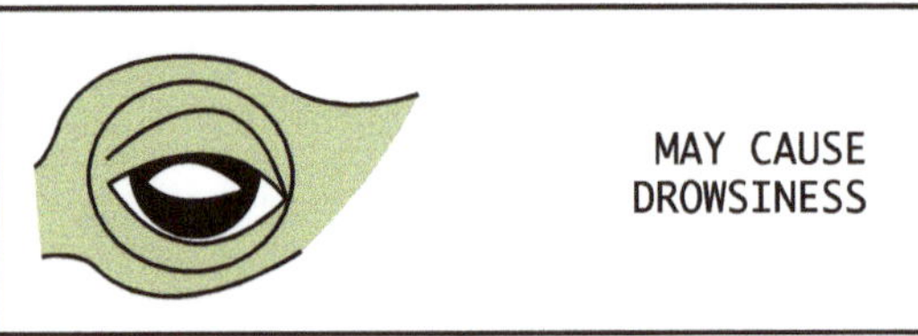

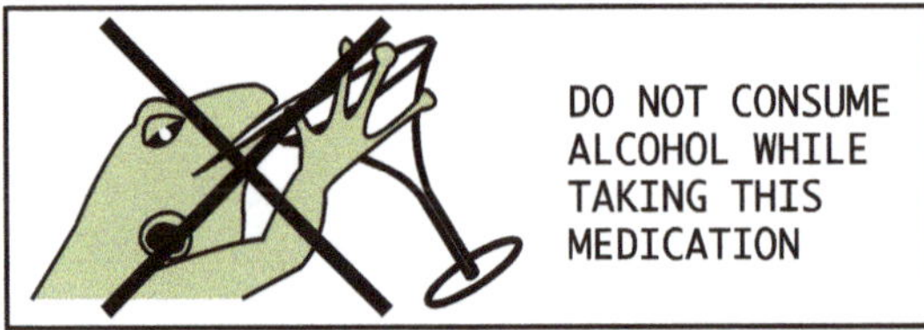

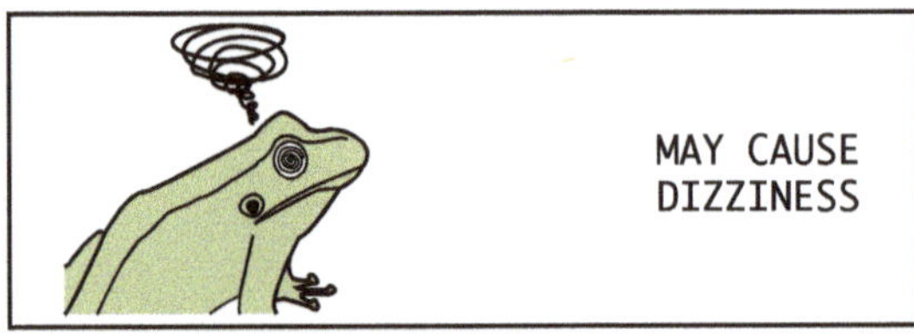

treat·ment (trēt′mənt) *n* **1** the act, manner, method of medical or surgical care **2** a written sketch outlining plot, characters, and action for a screenplay   **3** a process of alteration, often by chemical means

INFORMED CONSENT

PATIENT INSTRUCTIONS

TREATMENT IS MEANT ONLY
FOR ONE-TIME PROTECTION

1. Take two pills immediately (within 24 to 72 hours after exposure). Then take two more pills 12 hours after your first dose of pills.

2. Watch for pill danger signals:

caution! Abdominal pain (severe)
Chest pain (severe)
Headaches (severe)
Blurred vision
Severe leg pain (calf or thigh)

Complications are not likely with the short treatment, but if you experience any of the danger signs, you should either see your clinician right away or go to a hospital emergency room.

1. Get started immediately afterward with an acceptable ongoing method of protection.

2. The pill is approved by the Food and Drug Administration, but it is not approved for this one-time approach to preventing infection.

INFORMED CONSENT

I have read the above and am aware I am taking a one-time treatment intended to prevent infection after exposure. There is no guarantee that this will be successful. If unsuccessful, the pill could prove detrimental to future treatment.

_______________________   _______________________   _______________________
Patient's Signature   Witness   Date

DISTRIBUTION: WHITE = CHART   CANARY = PATIENT

map the state of illness
define the law of cure[10]

                                    purgative   expectorant   cathartic

                                                            treatment moves symptoms

inside to outside

                                        top to bottom

vital to non-vital organs
most recent to oldest sickness

———————

[10] I am ushered into a repurposed closet
   one chair   no windows
   a nurse repeats questions
   she reads off a form
   I nod   sweat through my pores
   the smell of last night's tequila permeates the room

cells gone wild

metal plates   cold fusion

the fingers of a tumor
are hard to uncurl

freeze for the cautery iron

shattering of an atom

immune to the flashbulb
rarely succumbing to the needle
reluctant to spill its secrets

incubate   inoculate   arrest
quarantine and kill

affect by radiant energy

                                        two pills
                                        every six hours
                                        no more than four times daily

                                        take with food

                    deer pellet BBs

                round with a pearly sheen

                oblong green and blue

soluble in water
spitting out fizz
liquid   chewable   gel cap

                                        calling out the gag reflex

                                                sliding down smooth

feel like yourself again

take control of your life

it´s not magic   it´s medication

one pill   one time   no mess

possible side effects include

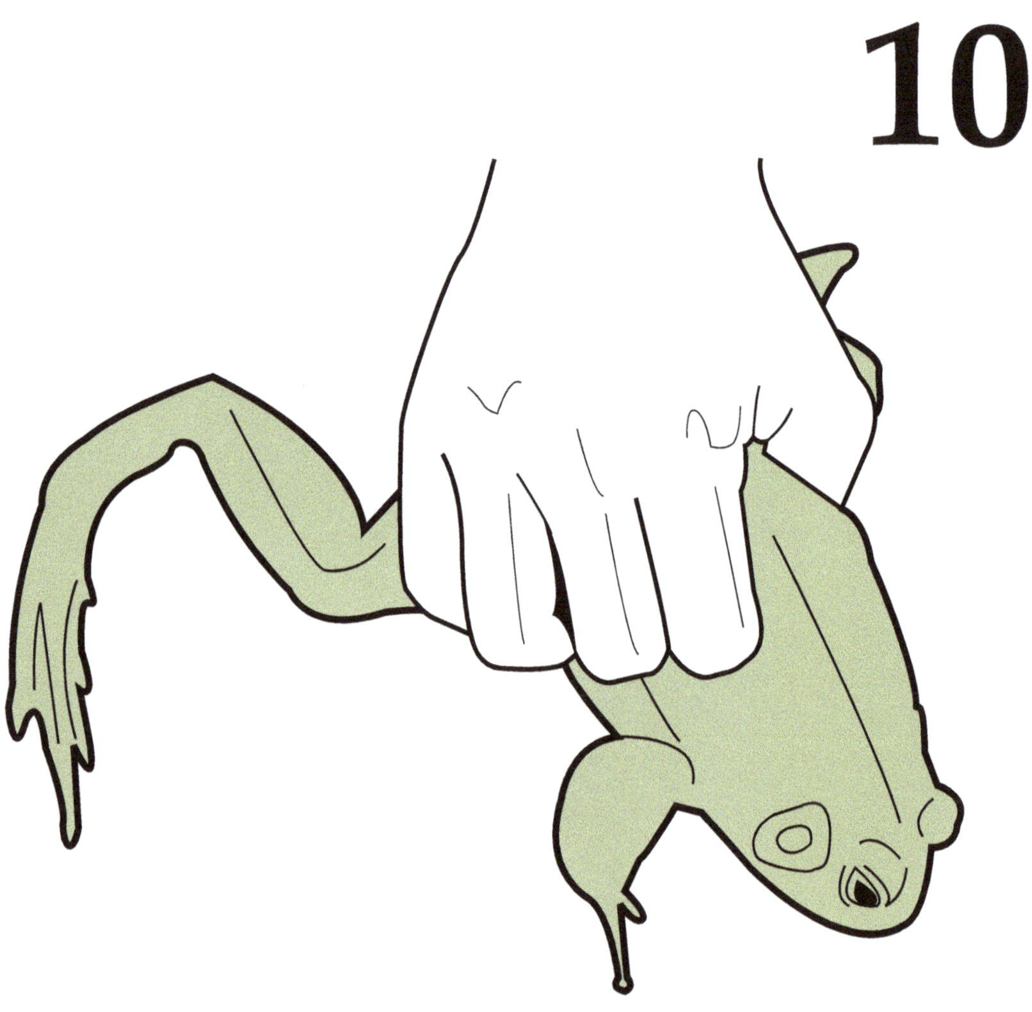

heal·ing (hēl´iŋ) *n* [[OE *hǣlan*]] **1** the act of causing an undesirable condition to be overcome **2** the process of curing, making sound or whole, or mending (a wound) **3** restoring to original purity or integrity

words part   waves part

                        seam across the sky

                        bodies bloom

dawn   a shedding of skin
sloughing off parts

                                        those stars are points piercing
                                        that sun an irritable sore

surely the moon festers
waiting for stars to shoot
for lightning to strike in vertical lines

                                        a flash deciphers skeletons

the sky the color of an infected wound

Leaps of Faith

The summer before I was in seventh grade, we moved into a house with a narrow strip of woods behind it. There was a shallow pond in the woods that swelled and shrank depending on what season it was. One day — it must have been in early summer or late spring — my mom and sister and I walked to the pond with a white plastic bucket. We filled the bucket with murky pond water and clumps of clear, green gelatinous frog eggs so that we could take them home and watch them hatch tadpoles and turn into frogs. We left the bucket on the wooden deck at the back of the house. A week or two later, the tadpoles hatched and swam around the bucket like tiny commas. One hot summer day, I noticed that the bucket had been knocked over and all of the water and tadpoles were gone. (Our calico cat seemed the most likely culprit.) What a tragedy! I walked down the wooden steps to the shaded space beneath the deck (where our woodpile was) and saw that a few of the tadpoles had landed in rainwater collected in an upturned blue plastic baby pool after slipping through the slats in the deck. I was so surprised to find them alive, and collected them back into the bucket. I went back up the steps to the deck and suddenly noticed black dots on the wooden surface of the deck. They were dried out tadpoles! I put a few drops of water on one of the dots and it began to swim around.

— Miranda Weiss

frogs jump into the water

shock   *ecstatic stasis*   *flushed ablutions*

salacious in the sunshine
none can measure the pleasure of floating

test the meniscus skin
ride the faith shield

view of white privates

freely given

rise above and hover

with movement there is healing

sun subsumed by moon
rivers washed in ink   etched soil

the shape of pain shifts

melts in shadow

a memory embedded in marrow
cased in bone

aroused consciousness

visible thunder   lightning song

there is peace

grow older   grow old
watch the pattern of the skin unfold

on the other side of panic
functioning with fear

before the end comes progress

in the clearing
silver and lush near dawn
residue of nocturnal fanfare   confetti strewn

storms rant   rage
leave dripping remains

layers of landscape uncovered

revelatory

in time   subdued

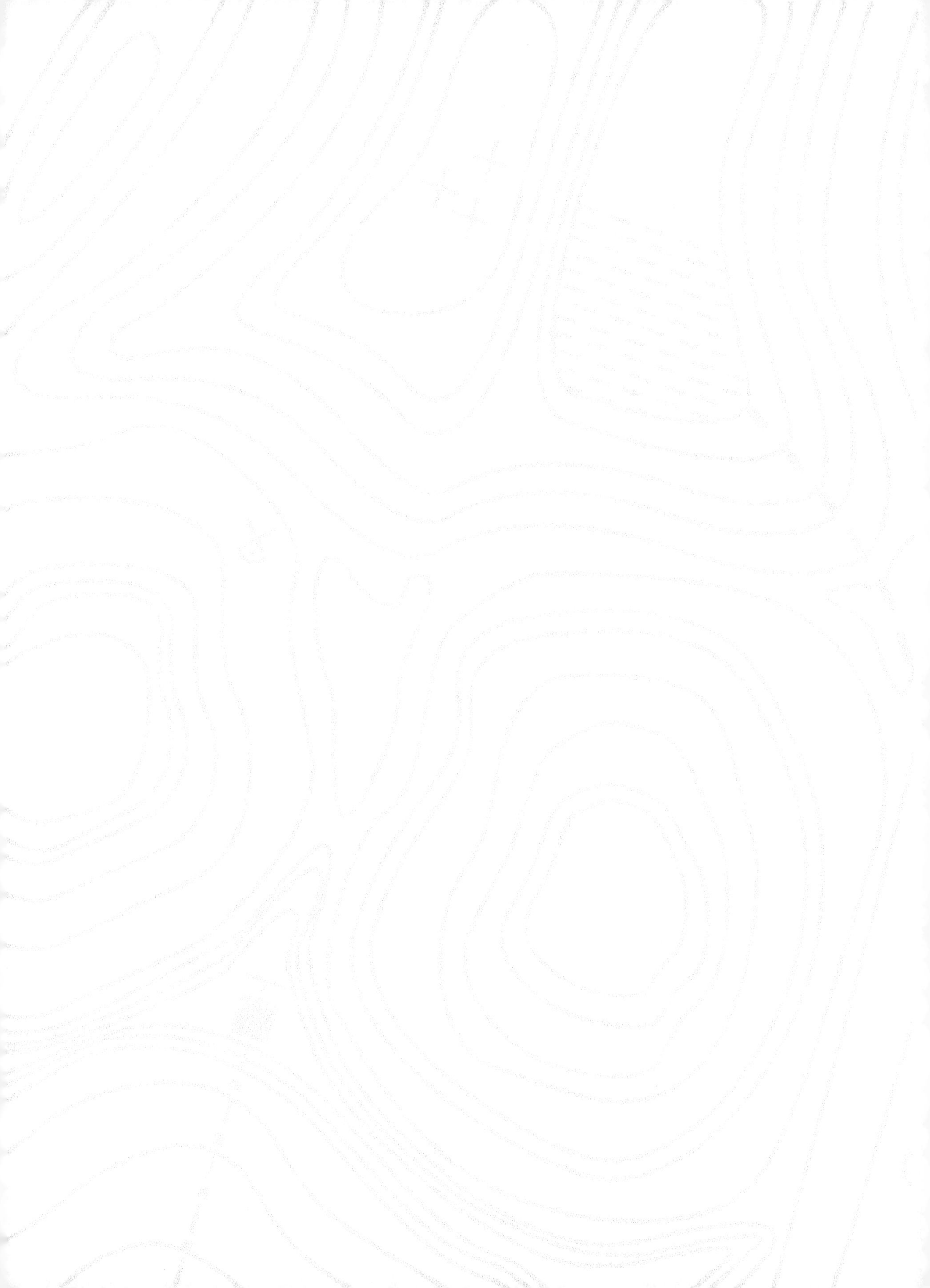

selected bibliography

CIBA Clinical Symposia, Vol. 32, No. 2. *Breast Lumps*. Courtney M. Townsend. Summit, NJ: CIBA Pharmaceutical Company, 1980.

Clemens, Samuel L. "The Jumping Frog of Calaveras County." In *The Jumping Frog and Other Stories and Sketches from the Exquisite Pen of Mr. Samuel L. Clemens*, 9-24. Mount Vernon, NY: The Peter Pauper Press, n.d.

Comen, Elizabeth. *All in Her Head: The Truth and Lies Early Medicine Taught Us About Women's Bodies and Why It Matters Today*. New York: HarperCollins Publishers, 2024.

Evans, Newton and others, eds. *The Home Physician and Guide to Health: A Treatise on the Prevention and Cure of Disease; Not Intended to Take the Place of the Family Physician, but to Aid the Reader in Coöperating with Him Intelligently*. Mountain View, CA: Pacific Press Publishing Association, 1923.

Field, Syd. *Screenplay: The Foundations of Writing*. New York: Dell Publishing, 1984.

Foucault, Michel. *The History of Sexuality, Volume 1: An Introduction*. New York: Vintage Books, 1990.

Fox, Charles D. *The Psychopathology of Hysteria*. Boston: The Gorham Press, 1913.

Greenhill, J.P. *Surgical Gynecology: A Handbook of Operative Surgery*. Chicago: The Year Book Publishers, Inc., 1952.

Hall, David H. *An Illustrated Dissection Guide To The Frog*. Tucson, AZ: RANACO, 1999.

Hubbard, Ruth. *The Politics of Women's Biology*. New Brunswick, NJ: Rutgers University Press, 1992.

Kroger, William S. and S. Charles Freed. *Psychosomatic Gynecology: Including Problems of Obstetrical Care*. Hollywood, CA: Wilshire Book Company, 1962.

Miller, Henry. *The World of Sex*. Paris: The Olympia Press, 1959.

Rayne Chamber of Commerce. *Rayne Chamber of Commerce Cookbook*. Rayne, LA: Independently Published, 2002.

Rowett, H.G.Q. *Dissection Guides: 1. The Frog.* New York: Holt, Rinehart and Winston, Inc., 1960.

Strong, Bryan and others. *Human Sexuality: Diversity in Contemporary America.* San Francisco: McGraw-Hill Higher Education, 2002.

Wallis, Lila A., ed. *Modern Breast & Pelvic Examinations: A Handbook for Health Professionals.* New York: National Council on Women's Health, Inc., 1996.

Whittles, Keith and Alice Goldie. *Concise Dictionary of Biology.* London: Tiger Books International, 1993.

acknowledgements

I am grateful to the Alfredo Cisneros del Moral Foundation and to Sandra Cisneros, who founded the organization in memory of her father, for a generous grant which afforded me the opportunity to spend one month in the Yucatan, separate from the rest of my life, to begin writing this book-length poem. Even more important than the monetary award, I am infinitely thankful for the confidence that receiving the grant gave me to embark on a project of this scope. I also appreciate the Fundación Valparaíso, an artists' residency program in Mojácar, Spain, for providing me with a studio space where I was able to lay out the pages of this piece and begin to visualize it as a three dimensional form. The residency allowed me the clarity of mind to write the preface to this poem, which had previously been so many knotted threads that were difficult to untangle. Beginning such a major undertaking as this piece also encouraged me to pursue the MFA in Creative Writing at San Francisco State University, where I was able to do a lot of the reading, research, and early writing in these pages. I am so grateful for those years at SFSU, the community that grew from my classes, and for Toni Mirosevich, whose transcendent workshops were an unforgettable adventure. Thank you Toni for your warmth and magic. Your *Writing About the Body* clearly was a huge influence on this poem. I am much obliged to Vanessa Kulzer Allen who was inspired in that class to get permission to visit a human cadaver lab at San Francisco City College. Thanks Vanessa, for inviting me to look inside bodies with you.

Living in San Francisco among a productive community of writers, artists, and thinkers, the breadth of this poem grew as I discussed my work with others. I genuinely appreciate everyone who took the time to examine this piece in progress, meet with me, and share their thoughts, particularly Truong Tran, Giancarlo Campagna, Rosemary Griggs, Brandon Brown, Beth Dungan, and John Weber. A very special thank you to Rachel Mercer, then a medical student, for reading and considering the poem from a doctor's standpoint. Additionally, I am grateful for the friends and family who told me about their experiences with frogs, and at my request, wrote them down, including my aunt Cristina Thomas, Marcia Brooks, Sama Abu Ayyash, and Matthew O'Donnell. Many kind thanks for the accounts by my mother Nora Barrera, Noel Kalenian, Bryan Mealer, Rachel Mercer, Paul Eveloff, and Miranda Weiss that are included in this book. Writing a piece that draws from research, I value the people who suggested that I consult specific books, notably Chet Walker, who referred me to Michel Foucault's *The History of Sexuality*. Unfortunately, I cannot remember who advised me to read Syd Field's *Screenwriting*, but if somehow you are reading this, I am indebted to you. Although it is an unconventional methodology for writing poetry, Field's technique for organizing text as discrete and mobile moments united by overlapping themes as a way of building a screenplay, aided me immensely in adapting the textbook format to contain this long poem.

This piece grew with me. It evolved over more than two decades, with periods of work followed by stretches untouched, only to become present, with another aspect of the whole claiming urgency again. Over the years and around the different places where I lived, I was fortunate to befriend generous souls who were willing to commit their energy to participate in live readings, poetry performances, of the piece. These brave people agreed to read aloud in front of others the selection that I gave them, unpracticed – Leaps of Faith, frog leg recipe, medical forms, Foucault quotes, definitions – usually without having seen the words beforehand, and often having little previous knowledge of *The Frog Poem Project*. Warmest regards for Layne Tanner, Jessica Lynn, and Sara Barr, owners of Lockhart Arts & Craft, for opening your doors to poetry, and for Sara, Nora Barrera, Laurel Coyle, Kevin Gillion, James Hush, Crystal Nuding, Kat Chuber, Dionne Robertson, Kate Schubert, Mike Shiplet, and Lee Simmons, who generously agreed to read. In an Airbnb outside Wimberly, Texas, I appreciate the all-female reading made possible by Kate, Elizabeth Roen, Iva Burmeister, Pansy Vore Price, and Alice Lam. In Chicago, Illinois, many thanks to Anne Novotvy, Rob Jeffries, Colleen O'Sullivan, Abra Aducci, Conor Oncken, Gene McHugh, and Abby Glogower. At the nascent beginning of writing this piece, I was honored to participate in Zeal, a reading series run by Brandon Brown in his apartment in San Francisco. I am beholden to all of you and am sincerely humbled by your support. Thank you for helping to make a poetry reading a collective, community event.

Beyond the bounds of this book, I call this long poem a project, in part, for the video and film footage that was shot while visiting frog festivals, often frequented by Hell's Angels and other bikers, and learning about the subculture, in pockets around the nation, that revolves around catching, sport jumping, cooking, eating, and even participating in beauty pageants with frogs. Considering my amphibian fears, it was a harrowing experience to attend these fairs, so I am indebted to Mark Lopez for going with me to New Orleans and driving us to the frog festival in Rayne, Louisiana, "Frog Capital of the World," and to my sister Valerie Rose Campbell, Kate Schubert, and Alice Lam for accompanying me to the Calaveras County Fair & Frog Jumping Jubilee, two years in a row. Thanks Kate, for even jumping a frog! Words cannot express the depth of gratitude I feel for my dearest lifelong friends, my best editor, Kate Schubert, and the visionary illustrator and designer of this book Alice Lam. It is impossible to recount everything that your skills and talents brought to these pages. I am gratified and humbled by your unwavering belief in me and in the value of this project. Finally, the most special thanks to Jason Costanzo, my husband, my soulmate, the love of my life – forever and always.

…and to anyone who has made it this far, thank you kindly for reading…

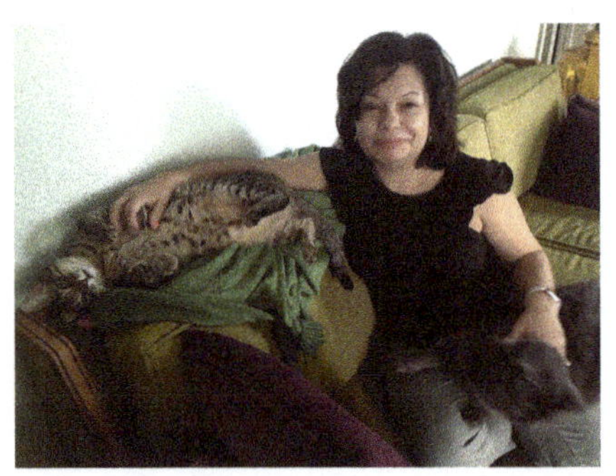

Nicolette Costanzo is a former Fulbright Scholar to Iceland and writer in residence at Fundación Valparaíso in Mojácar, Spain. Early pieces (under her maiden name Nicole Pollentier) were included in *Bird Dog, Fourteen Hills,* and others, as well as in Latina poetry anthologies *¡Floricanto Sí!* (Penguin) and *Daughters of the Fifth Sun* (Riverhead / Putnam). With an MFA in Creative Writing from San Francisco State University and an MA in Curatorial Studies from Bard College, Nicolette utilizes poetry as a research methodology and writes long-form pieces that exceed the boundaries of genres and disciplines. She lives in Lockhart, Texas, with her husband and two cats.

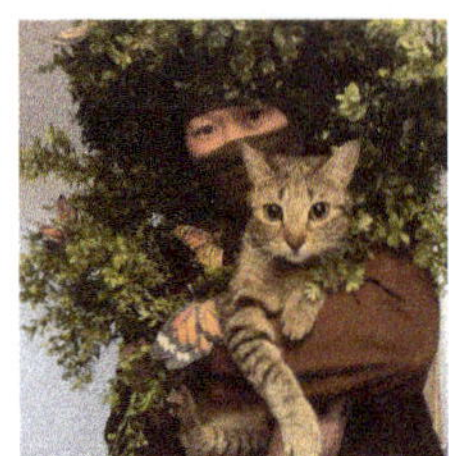

Alice Lam is a textile designer and mixed-media artist based in New York City's East Village, working under the studio name *circlealine*. Along with notable commercial outlets, her work has appeared in publications such as *Centurion, Interior Design, Kolaj, Raw Fury,* and *Uppercase Magazine.*

The Frog Poem Project is an expanding, accessible community effort. If you enjoyed this book, please consider sharing it or stashing a copy in a public place for someone else to discover. Tag @thefrogpoemproject and follow us on Instagram as we announce upcoming readings / events and document your contributions. Additional copies are available through the link in bio.

name	/email	location	date